HAMZA LAAOUAMRI

Whispers of What Could Have Been

First edition

This book was professionally typeset on Reedsy.
Find out more at reedsy.com

Contents

Chapter 1

The Gilded Hour

The sun, a benevolent artist, was washing the sky in strokes of saffron and rose, its final light spilling through the skeletal fingers of a London plane tree. Harrison sat on the park bench, a fixture of iron and weary patience, feeling the day's warmth leach from the air. The in-between time. Not quite day, not yet night. He had always been drawn to these liminal spaces, the thresholds of existence where one thing was becoming another. His own life felt like a long, drawn-out dusk.

Around him, the park breathed with a gentle, rhythmic life. The distant, percussive splash of the central fountain was a constant heartbeat against the low hum of city traffic, a sound so familiar it was merely a texture of silence. A soft breeze, carrying the scent of damp earth and the faintest ghost of diesel, stirred the hair at his temples. He felt its touch, a cool caress against the day's accumulated tension, and his own breathing deepened, slowing to the park's unhurried pulse.

He watched a young couple share a carton of noodles on a nearby bench, their laughter a bright, uncomplicated sound that seemed to catch the last of the sun's rays. Their movements were easy, fluid, their heads leaning together in a small conspiracy of joy. Harrison's gaze drifted past them to the children chasing pigeons near the fountain, their shrieks of delight sharp and fleeting as the birds themselves. He felt a pang, not of envy, but of a profound and hollow wondering. What did it feel like to inhabit a moment so completely? To be so utterly present in the small, tactile realities of one's own happiness?

His hand rested on the worn leather of the briefcase beside him, its surface smooth and cool beneath his palm. Inside were contracts, projections, the architecture of a life built on careful calculations and the managed expectations of others. It felt impossibly heavy. The lingering taste of burnt coffee, the day's third, was a bitter film on his tongue. He ran his tongue over his teeth, a small, unconscious act of trying to wipe the slate clean.

A vendor pushed a cart along the perimeter path, the sweet, smoky aroma of roasted chestnuts beginning to curl into the evening air. The scent was thick with a nostalgia for a life Harrison had only observed. A life of simple pleasures, of shared warmth on a cooling evening, of hands intertwined. He saw the shadows stretching from the base of the trees, long, dark fingers reaching across the manicured lawns. They were like his own thoughts, elongating in the quiet, touching everything with a shade of introspection, a hint of what was absent. He could feel the solid bench beneath him, the vibration of a distant underground train a faint tremor through the soles of his shoes, yet he felt untethered, a ghost observing a world of substance.

Is a life defined by its visible structure, he wondered, or by the invisible currents of joy that flow through it? Are we the sum of our achievements, the solid things we can point to, or are we the collection of a thousand unremembered moments—a shared laugh, the warmth of a hand, the simple peace of watching a sunset paint the sky? The gilded light caught the spray of the fountain, turning the water into a cascade of liquid gold. A fleeting moment of impossible beauty. He watched it, his heart a slow, steady drum in the cavern of his chest, feeling the profound silence that separates the life one has from the life one imagines.

Chapter 2

The Echo of Unspoken Words

The gold had deepened to bronze, and the bronze was now bruising into violet along the serrated edge of the city skyline. The park lamps flickered to life, one by one, casting pools of honeyed, artificial light onto the paths, turning the remaining daylight into a thin, ethereal mist. Harrison drew the collar of his coat closer to his neck, the fine wool a soft friction against his skin. A definite chill had arrived, a harbinger of the night, carrying on its breath the damp, mineral scent of the fountain's spray and the clean, sharp fragrance of clipped lawns.

The couple on the other bench had fallen silent. They were not speaking, yet the space between them hummed with conversation. Her head rested on his shoulder; his arm was a secure, warm line around her. Harrison watched the simple, profound architecture of their comfort, the easy stillness that spoke of a thousand conversations already had, and a thousand more to come. He could not hear a word, yet he felt he understood everything. It was a language spoken in the subtle shift of weight, the gentle rise and fall of their breathing.

He closed his eyes for a moment, letting the soundscape of the park wash over him. The city's drone, the distant wail of a siren slicing through the evening, the dry rustle of a discarded newspaper skittering across the flagstones. And in his mind, he began to furnish a silence of his own. He imagined a small kitchen, bathed in the soft glow of a single pendant light. The aroma of chamomile tea, steamy and floral, rising from two mugs. The solid, comforting weight of one of them in his hands, its heat seeping into his palms. Across the table, a face, soft in the low light, listening.

And what would they speak of? Not of profit margins or market futures. Perhaps the comical absurdity of a colleague's tie, the simple satisfaction of a garden weed pulled, or the quiet miracle of a bird's nest discovered in the eaves. Nothing of consequence. Everything of importance. The thought unfolded with a gentle, aching clarity. He had spent a lifetime mastering the art of the declarative statement, the persuasive argument, the definitive word. But he had never learned the grammar of quiet communion.

His own heart beat a steady, solitary rhythm in his chest, a clock ticking in an empty room. He felt a sudden, sharp thirst, and the memory of the day's stale coffee was replaced by the imagined, clean taste of cool water. A life, he mused, is perhaps measured not in its great pronouncements, but in its shared whispers. The meaning is not in the words themselves, but in the spaces between them, the comfortable silences where two people can simply *be*, their presence a quiet affirmation of the other.

He opened his eyes. The couple was standing now, gathering their things. They moved with an unhurried, synchronized grace, and then they were gone, their departure leaving a void in the tableau of the park. The bench they had occupied was now just an empty shape under the lamplight, and the silence they left behind was not full, but hollow. Harrison sat perfectly still, listening to the echo of unspoken words from a life he had only just begun to imagine.

Chapter 3

A Tapestry of Footsteps

The violet sky was now sewn with the first, timid stars, pinpricks of cold light in the deepening fabric of night. Across the street, the cheerful, beckoning glow of shop windows began to die. A bakery, a bookstore, a small boutique—each one blinked out, leaving behind a darker, more anonymous facade. With each extinguished light, the park seemed to contract, pulling its shadows closer, the world beyond its iron railings receding into a muted sketch. The air grew heavier, thick with the promise of rain, and carried the scent of cool, damp stone and the faint, savory ghost of fried onions from a closing takeaway stand.

Harrison's attention shifted to the flow of humanity along the park's main artery. A river of footsteps, each with its own distinct cadence, its own story. The sharp, hurried clicks of a woman's heels on the flagstones spoke of purpose, of a destination eagerly sought or a duty to be met. The slow, rhythmic shuffle of an elderly man, his form a stooped silhouette against the distant streetlights, told a tale of time measured and journeys nearing their end. A child, breaking free from his mother's hand, added a flurry of chaotic, joyful patter, a sound that was pure, unwritten potential.

He felt the cold of the iron bench begin to seep through the layers of his clothing, a deep, patient chill that seemed to emanate from the earth itself. He clasped his hands in his lap, the skin of his knuckles cool and dry to the touch. Each person who passed was a vessel of a life as complex and vast as his own. They were heading home, perhaps, to lighted windows, to waiting arms, to the mundane and sacred rituals of an evening meal. Or maybe they were heading into a loneliness as profound as the one he felt settling around him. There was no way to know. They were just threads, crossing his path for a moment before continuing on their own trajectory into the vast, intricate tapestry of the city.

Did any of them, he wondered, carry a similar phantom life within them? A life of quiet longing that ran parallel to the one they were visibly living? The man with the determined stride—did he ever dream of a slower pace, of a morning with no agenda? The woman pulling the shopping trolley, her face etched with fatigue—did she imagine a life of unburdened leisure? It struck him then that perhaps this was the shared, secret condition of humanity: to walk one path while forever glancing down the myriad of roads not taken. We are all, in our own way, haunted by the ghosts of the lives we nearly lived.

The air tasted clean, with a subtle metallic tang that hinted at the coming rain. His own heartbeat was a quiet, internal metronome, marking time against the varied rhythms of the passing footsteps. The question arose, unbidden and quiet as the night. Is a life a single, forward narrative, or is it a collection of infinite possibilities, with the one we inhabit being no more real or valid than the ones we can only imagine? The path he was on felt so solid, so irrefutable, paved with decades of choices. Yet, in this moment, it felt as thin as a shadow, just one of many that he might have cast. He watched the last few figures recede into the gloom, their footsteps fading into the city's ceaseless murmur, leaving him in the profound stillness of his own singular, untrodden what-if.

Chapter 4

The Silent Logic of Trees

The air had grown heavy, a weighted blanket of humidity that promised but did not yet deliver rain. It carried the rich, loamy perfume of damp soil and the darker, almost fungal scent of decaying leaves in the park's shaded corners. The world had shrunk to the circumference of the lamplight around Harrison's bench. Beyond it, the darkness was absolute, swallowing sound and shape. He felt as if he were on a small, illuminated stage, the drama of his thoughts the only performance of the night.

His gaze lifted from the empty path to the magnificent plane tree that presided over this small quadrant of the park. Lit from below by the orange glow of a park lamp, its familiar daytime aspect was gone. The light cast strange, theatrical shadows upward, turning the pale, mottled bark into a landscape of miniature hills and valleys and making the leaves a translucent, almost alien green. It looked like something from a dream, a silent, watchful giant.

A lone jogger emerged from the gloom, his breath preceding him in rhythmic, silver plumes. The soft, percussive thud of his trainers on the asphalt was a disciplined, relentless sound. He passed through Harrison's circle of light and disappeared back into the darkness, the sound of his effort fading slowly. The man's purpose was so clear, so linear: to move from one point to another, to measure his existence in strides and heartbeats. Harrison recognized the feeling. It was the story of his own life—a relentless forward momentum, a constant measuring of progress.

But the tree. The tree did not move. Its journey was not horizontal, but vertical. It did not strive; it simply grew. Its roots, a vast, unseen network, delved deep into the earth, drawing strength from the darkness, from the quiet, hidden places. Its branches reached for the light, not with ambition, but with a kind of patient, irrefutable instinct. It was a life of profound, silent logic. Harrison ran a hand along the cold, damp iron of the bench, the texture gritty beneath his fingertips. The tree's existence was its own justification. It asked for no validation, presented no quarterly reports. It simply was.

What, he wondered, were his own roots? Where did they draw their nourishment from? The question unsettled him. He had built a life that was all canopy—a wide, impressive spread of visible achievements. But the unseen foundation, the part of him that was meant to be anchored in the simple, life-giving soil of human connection, of quiet contentment... he feared it was a shallow, desperate tangle, forever seeking purchase in dry, unforgiving ground.

The taste in his mouth was of nothing but the cool, damp air. He drew a deep breath, and it felt like drinking something pure and ancient. A single, heavy drop of condensation fell from a leaf high above and landed on the back of his hand. The touch was startlingly cold, a tiny, fleeting shock that made his awareness sharpen. He looked at the glistening bead of water on his skin, a perfect, temporary jewel. The tree was not idle; it was a participant in the world, gathering the night's moisture, breathing in what the city exhaled, a quiet, tireless engine of life. Harrison sat motionless, feeling the immense, unhurried life of the tree beside him, a presence that asked nothing of him but offered a silent, compelling alternative to the frantic logic of his own world.

Chapter 5

The Geography of Belonging

The rain began not as a decision, but as a slow, thoughtful surrender. A single, fat drop landed on the leather of his briefcase, leaving a dark, star-shaped mark. Then another on a leaf overhead, with a sound like a soft tap on a drum. Soon a gentle, persistent patter filled the air, a thousand tiny, random notes composing a single, cohesive melody. The world smelled of petrichor—that ancient, sacred scent of rain meeting dry earth—and the sharp, clean perfume of wet asphalt.

Harrison did not move. He tilted his head back slightly, letting the cool, fine mist kiss his face. The droplets felt like a release, a soft absolution for a day, a life, lived under pressure. The light from the park lamps now seemed to bleed into the damp air, each one surrounded by a fuzzy, golden halo, turning the familiar scene into a hazy, impressionistic painting. The paths glistened, reflecting the light in wavering, distorted lines, as if the solid ground had become uncertain of its own form.

From the deep shadows at the edge of the path, a figure emerged: a man in a heavy coat, his head bent against the weather, holding the taut leash of a small terrier that trotted with brisk importance. As they passed through the light, the dog glanced at Harrison, its dark, intelligent eyes holding a moment of frank, uncomplicated curiosity before being pulled along. They were a single unit of purpose, moving through the rain towards a presumed warmth, a dry floor, a closed door. Towards home.

The word resonated in the quiet, rain-filled space of Harrison's mind. *Home*. He had a house, of course. A place of clean lines, polished surfaces, and art chosen for its investment potential. A place where silence was the default setting. But was it a home? He tried to conjure the sensory details of it now—the faint, chemical scent of the cleaning service, the cool, sterile touch of the marble countertops, the precise, architectural echo of his own footsteps on the hardwood floors. It was a structure, an address, a container for his life. It was not a home.

A home, he began to think, was a different geography altogether. Its coordinates were not marked by street signs, but by the accumulation of lived moments. It smelled of baking bread, or of one particular person's perfume lingering in a room. It tasted of a thousand shared meals, the simple, nourishing flavor of soup on a cold day. Its soundtrack was the comfortable creak of a familiar floorboard, the gentle hum of a radiator, the sound of a key turning in a lock that meant the day's solitude was over. He imagined the feeling of sinking into a worn armchair, the fabric molded by years of use, a silent testament to rest and reprieve.

A shiver, born of both the evening's chill and the starkness of his thoughts, traced a path down his spine. The fine wool of his overcoat was becoming heavy with moisture, a damp weight on his shoulders. Has a man truly lived, he wondered, if he has never had a place to return to? Not just a place to sleep, but a place where the very walls seem to exhale a quiet welcome, where one is known so completely that no performance is required. He had built a life that was weatherproof, secure, a fortress against uncertainty. But in doing so, he had locked out the very elements that might have made it a sanctuary. He remained on the bench, a solitary island in the steadily falling rain, feeling the profound, unbreachable distance between the house he owned and the home he had never known.

Chapter 6

Ghosts in the Rain

The rain had lost its gentleness and was now a steady, relentless percussion on the world's roof. It drummed on the broad leaves of the plane tree, slicked the iron armrests of the bench, and formed a shimmering, ever-moving skin on the asphalt paths. Harrison was soaked through. The fine fabric of his suit, a carefully constructed armor against the world, was now a heavy, sodden shroud, clinging to his skin. He had long since passed the point of discomfort and entered a state of strange, detached acceptance. The cold was no longer just on his skin, but in his marrow, a deep, resonant chill that seemed to emanate from his own hollow core.

His gaze was fixed on the children's playground, set back from the path under the dark, dripping canopy of an oak. During the day, it was a kinetic explosion of color and sound. Now, it was a skeletal wreck, an archipelago of cheerful colors in a sea of night. The rain had washed it clean, and the wet surfaces of the slide and climbing frame gleamed under the distant park lights like polished bone. In the slight, shifting wind, one of the swings moved with a slow, ghostly rhythm, its chains issuing a faint, metallic complaint. *Creek... croak... creek... croak*. The sound was lonely, mechanical, the antithesis of a child's carefree joy.

Yet, in the steady drumming of the rain, he could almost hear the ghosts of laughter. He could almost see small, brightly-colored rain boots splashing in the puddles that were forming near the base of the slide. And with a clarity that made his chest ache, he could almost feel the phantom weight of a small, trusting hand in his own. He imagined the sensation—the surprising strength in those tiny fingers, the warmth of them, a small, human anchor in the vastness of the world. He pictured himself lifting a child, face bright with exhilaration, onto the swing, the sound of their delighted squeal cutting through the gray air.

What is a life, if not a collection of such small, irreplaceable textures? The rough bark of a tree under a child's curious fingers, the soft down of their hair against your cheek, the slightly sweet, milky scent of their breath. He had built a world of smooth, hard surfaces, of things that could be quantified and insured. But he had no inventory of these small, sacred moments. He had no one to leave his stories to, no one to inherit the geography of his own heart. His legacy was written in ink on paper, not in the living memory of another human being.

The taste of rain was on his lips, clean and cold and utterly neutral. It had no memory, no story. It simply was. He felt his own heart beating, a slow, heavy thud against his ribs, a lonely drum keeping time with the rain and the creaking swing. Is a person's existence validated by those who love them, he wondered, or can a solitary life, however successful, ever truly feel complete? He looked at his own hand, resting on his knee. It was pale and empty, the skin puckered from the damp, the rain collecting in the small valleys between his knuckles. A hand that had signed contracts and shaken on deals, but had never been held just for the simple, profound comfort of it. It held nothing now but the falling rain.

Chapter 7

The Lit Window

The rain had settled into the city's bones. It flowed in glistening rivulets along the gutters, dripped with a somber, metronomic regularity from the tips of leaves, and turned the air into a fine, breathable liquid. Harrison no longer felt the individual drops; the sensation had merged into a single, encompassing state of being—wet, cold, profoundly still. His own body felt like a stone at the bottom of a river, the world flowing around it, its internal warmth a distant, fading memory.

His gaze, slow and heavy, drifted from the dark, saturated green of the park to the street beyond. The shops were dark voids, their signs unlit, their windows reflecting the wet, empty street like obsidian mirrors. But across the road, one square of light stood in defiant opposition to the night. A small, all-night cafe. Its window was a warm, golden rectangle, fogged from the inside with the accumulated breath and steam of human life. It was a beacon, a promise of a world that was not cold and dark.

He watched the blurred silhouettes moving within, their motions softened and made dreamlike by the condensation. He could just make out the form of a barista, moving with efficient grace behind the counter. A couple sat at a small table near the glass, their heads inclined towards each other, their shapes occasionally merging into one. He couldn't hear their voices, but he could imagine the sound—a low, intimate murmur, a counterpoint to the steady drumming of the rain. He could almost smell the rich, dark-chocolate aroma of fresh coffee, the sweet, buttery scent of baked pastries, scents that promised warmth and simple, restorative pleasure. The only taste in his own mouth was the clean, mineral tang of the rain.

A hand from inside wiped a clear circle on the steamed glass, a temporary porthole into that other world. For a fleeting moment, Harrison saw a young woman's face, illuminated and unguarded, as she laughed at something the person opposite her had said. Her expression was a small, perfect composition of uncomplicated joy. Then the circle fogged over again, and she was gone, dissolved back into the golden haze. The brief, sharp clarity of the image left an ache in Harrison's chest that was more profound than the physical cold.

We build our lives, he thought, choosing what to let in and what to keep out. He had built walls of glass—sleek, modern, and impenetrable, allowing him to see the world while remaining untouched by it. He had mistaken observation for participation. This little cafe window, clouded and imperfect, was a more honest barrier. It separated the warmth from the cold, the inside from the outside, the participant from the spectator. He could feel the unyielding hardness of the bench beneath him, the rough, cold texture of his sodden sleeve against his cheek where he rested his head on his hand.

What is sustenance? Is it the meticulously crafted, nutritionally balanced meal eaten in a silent, empty dining room? Or is it a simple cup of coffee, imbued with the warmth of shared space, the nourishment of human presence? He felt a hunger so deep and so vast it had nothing to do with food. It was a hunger for the steam on a window, for the sound of a stranger's laughter, for the simple, profound communion of being inside, looking out at the rain, instead of outside, looking in. The golden light of the window pulsed softly in the dark, a silent, steady heartbeat of a life he was not living.

Chapter 8

The Currency of Moments

The rain had begun to soften its voice, descending from a persistent drumbeat to a hushed, conspiratorial whisper. It was a sound that seemed to encourage introspection, drawing the world into a smaller, more intimate frame. Harrison felt the cold not as an attack from the outside, but as a condition of his own blood, a deep, cellular chill that had settled in his very core. His breathing was shallow, visible in the damp air as faint, ghostly plumes. Each exhalation felt like a small surrender, a letting go of some essential warmth.

A thought, pragmatic and sharp, finally pierced the dense fog of his reflection: *This is foolish*. The sentence formed with the clear, cold logic that had governed his entire adult life. He was a man of resources, of solutions. To sit here, inviting illness, was an indulgence in a kind of misery he had spent decades systematically eliminating from his existence. The answer was in his pocket.

With stiff, chilled fingers, he reached inside his sodden coat and retrieved his phone. The device was a perfect, seamless slab of glass and metal, its cold, hard reality a stark contrast to the organic chaos of the rain-soaked park. It felt impossibly foreign in his hand. He pressed the side button. The screen flared to life, an aggressive, sterile white light that momentarily blinded him, making the gentle gloom of the park seem like a haven.

Before the icons and notifications populated the screen, for a single, stark second, the dark glass acted as a mirror. He saw his own face, hollowed out by the phone's light from below, rain-streaked and pale. The face of a stranger. This was the man whose name commanded attention in boardrooms, whose opinion could shift fortunes. But the eyes staring back from the screen were vacant, haunted by a poverty the world could not see.

Then the world rushed in. Emails flagged as urgent. Missed calls from three continents. A stream of market data scrolling in a relentless, coded language. This was the currency of his life—a constant flow of information, of obligation, of profit and loss. He could, with a few taps on this cold surface, summon a heated car to his exact location, purchase a flight, liquidate an asset. He held in his hand a tool of immense power in the world he inhabited.

And yet.

His gaze drifted back to the cafe window, to that small, warm rectangle of light. The wealth he possessed could buy the entire building. It could not buy him a single, genuine moment of the life within it. He had spent his entire life mastering one economy, only to find himself a beggar in another. The currency of that other world was not traded on any exchange. It was a currency of shared glances, of comfortable silences, of hands held under a small table, of moments spent and invested in the simple, unrepeatable present. He had hoarded his time, spent it meticulously on acquiring a fortune, and in doing so, had bankrupted his soul.

His thumb, wrinkled and pale, hovered over the screen. He could end this. He could go back to the world of dry clothes and warm rooms and silent, orderly solitude. But for the first time, the alternative felt less like a solution and more like a surrender. With a quiet, deliberate motion, he pressed the button again. The screen went dark. He slipped the phone back into the wet confines of his pocket, its potential energy now just a cold, heavy weight. It was a small act, seen by no one, but it felt like the first truly defiant choice he had made in years.

Chapter 9

The Clearing

The end of the rain was not an event, but a process of subtraction. The world grew quieter by degrees. The insistent drumming on the leaves softened to a gentle patter, then to a sporadic, thoughtful drip, until finally, the only sound was the patient ticking of water falling from the high branches onto the sodden earth below. A profound silence descended, a quiet so deep it seemed to have a physical weight. The air, washed clean of the city's grit, tasted of ozone and wet stone, a flavor of pure, elemental renewal.

As if on cue, the thick blanket of clouds began to fray at the edges. A tear in the fabric of the night revealed a sliver of impossible light—the moon, sharp and silver and utterly indifferent. Its cold, clean light spilled onto the park, transforming the scene once more. The puddles on the path were no longer dark voids, but pools of liquid mercury, perfectly mirroring the newly cleared sky. Every wet leaf, every blade of grass, was suddenly edged in a fine, silver filigree. The world, which had been a hazy watercolor, was now a stark, beautiful etching.

From the far end of the park, a new sound emerged. A rhythmic, abrasive scraping. A municipal worker, anonymous in a high-visibility jacket that shone a ghostly yellow in the moonlight, was sweeping the gutters with a long, stiff-bristled broom. *Shush. Shush. Shush*. The sound was methodical, hypnotic. The man worked with a slow, deliberate grace, his movements economical and certain. He was not wrestling with the debris, but simply coaxing it along, clearing a path, restoring a small, forgotten corner of the world to order.

Harrison watched him, transfixed. The man's task was simple, tangible, its results immediate and undeniable. He was not contemplating what might have been; he was dealing with what was—the accumulated litter of a single day. A thought, clear and sharp as the moonlight, settled in Harrison's mind. He had been living his life as if it were a complex, theoretical problem to be solved. He had analyzed it, projected it, lamented its flawed design. But he had never simply swept it clean.

He had let the debris of unmet expectations, of silent resentments, of hollow ambitions, pile up in the gutters of his soul until he could no longer see the path for the clutter. The rain had been a kind of baptism, washing away the noise. Now, in the aftermath, he was seeing the landscape of his own life with a terrifying, liberating clarity. The loneliness was not a phantom; it was a real thing. The emptiness was not a mood; it was a space he had meticulously, if unconsciously, built.

He felt the rough, damp wool of his own sleeve against his hand.

He felt the solid, cold certainty of the bench beneath him. His heart, which had been a dull ache, now beat with a slow, quiet steadiness. It was the rhythm of a man who had finally stopped running. For the first time all evening, he was not mourning the life he hadn't lived. He was simply inhabiting, completely and without judgment, the one he had. The worker finished his section of the path and moved on, his rhythmic sweeping fading into the new silence. Harrison sat in the stark, clean moonlight, looking at the dark, glistening path before him, feeling the profound, still-point of a world washed clean.

Chapter 10

The Gravity of Standing

The silence that followed the rain was a living thing. It was composed of the slow, patient drip of water from leaf to leaf, the soft sigh of the breeze through the newly washed branches, and the immense, quiet hum of the city asleep. The moon, now unobscured, was a disc of polished silver, and its light was not a gentle wash, but a sharp, defining blade. It carved the world into two distinct entities: things that were illuminated, and things that were in shadow. There was no longer any room for ambiguity.

Harrison felt the change not just in the air, but in his own body. The dampness of his clothes was no longer a miserable shroud, but simply a fact. A physical sensation. He could feel the precise, cool outline of the wet fabric against his skin, the heavy drag of the wool. He could feel the unyielding iron of the bench beneath him, a solid point of contact with a world that suddenly felt intensely, undeniably real. The scent of the air was the scent of possibility—of wet earth ready for new growth, of clean stone wiped free of yesterday's dust.

He looked at his hands, lying open on his knees. In the moonlight, they were pale and stark, a map of veins and tendons. They were his hands. They had built a life of careful, lonely precision. They had signed the documents, held the briefcases, turned the keys in the locks of empty rooms. He had always seen them as instruments of his ambition. Now, for the first time, he saw them simply as hands. Capable. Empty. Waiting.

The door of the little cafe across the street opened, and a bell, a tiny, clear note of silver, tinkled in the vast quiet. A brief, warm wave of sound—a snatch of music, a burst of laughter—spilled out onto the wet pavement along with a momentary, fragrant cloud of coffee and warm sugar. It was not a painful reminder of his exclusion. It was an invitation. A statement of fact: warmth existed in the world. Connection existed. It was not a dream from another life; it was right there, across the street, a tangible place.

A new thought, simple and profound, arose from the deep stillness within him. It was no longer a question of what his life could have been. The only relevant question was the one the moonlight was asking: *What is it, now?* A life, he realized, is not a static monument to be judged upon its completion. It is a living thing, a process. Even a foundation built of stone and solitude could be the beginning of something else. A garden could be planted in its courtyard. A window could be cut into its walls.

Slowly, deliberately, he moved. The motion began in his core, a conscious decision that traveled through his stiff, cold limbs. He placed his hands flat on the bench beside him, the wet, gritty iron a shock of cold to his palms. He pushed. His muscles, long dormant, protested. His joints ached. The sound was a soft, wet tearing as his clothes peeled away from the bench. And then he was on his feet.

He stood. The simple act had a profound gravity to it. He felt his own weight on the earth, the solid ground beneath his shoes. He was no longer a seated observer, a ghost in the machine of the park. He was a vertical being in a horizontal world, a figure of potential energy. The path ahead, slick and black and streaked with the moon's silver, led out of the park. It led in two directions. He stood, for a long moment, simply feeling the choice in his bones, a quiet, terrifying, and distinctly hopeful thing.

Chapter 11

The First Step

To stand was to be a landmark in one's own life. Harrison felt the full, simple truth of it in the pull of his muscles, in the solid connection of his feet to the wet, unyielding earth. The world, viewed from this new, vertical perspective, was subtly altered. The bench was now a thing below him, a piece of his past. The path stretched before him, not as a picture to be observed, but as a space to be navigated. His shadow, cast long and thin by the high moon, pointed the way forward, a dark, silent arrow leading out of the park's quiet heart.

The air itself felt different now that he was moving through it. A slight breeze, born in the high, empty canyons of the city, met his face, and the touch of it on his cold, damp skin was a startling, clean sensation. It carried the scent of wet leaves and the distant, metallic tang of the sleeping city. He could feel the slight friction of his sodden trousers around his knees with each movement, the squelch of his expensive leather shoes, now ruined and waterlogged. These were not distractions, but affirmations. They were the undeniable, tactile proof of his own presence in this singular, unrepeatable moment.

He reached the edge of the park, where the manicured quiet met the hard, geometric reality of the street. To his left, the road led back towards the familiar architecture of his life—the silent apartment, the sterile office, the life that was a fortress of his own making. To his right, the road curved away towards the glowing window of the cafe and, beyond that, the unknown. The choice was not between two destinations, but between two ways of being. It was the choice between the familiar grammar of his past and the terrifying, unwritten language of a potential future.

He paused, one foot on the park's flagstones, the other on the curb of the city street, occupying the threshold. He listened. The world offered no guidance. There was only the quiet hum of a distant electrical substation, the hiss of a passing car on the wet asphalt, the slow, steady rhythm of his own heartbeat in his ears. The taste in his mouth was of clean, cool air, a palate wiped clean.

What is a life, he thought, but a series of single steps? We fool ourselves into believing it is a grand, sweeping narrative, but it is built atom by atom, moment by moment, choice by choice. The past was a ghost, the future a vapor. All he truly owned was this single, solid instant. The decision to stand. The will to move. He was not the sum of his regrets, nor the architect of a flawless future. He was only a man, standing in the rain-washed moonlight, with a path before him.

He lifted his gaze from the glistening street to the vast, silent sky, where a few tenacious stars held their cold, distant light. He drew a deep, slow breath, filling his lungs with the clean, damp air of the new, unsettled world. And then, he took a step.

www.ingramcontent.com/pod-product-compliance
Lightning Source LLC
La Vergne TN
LVHW101618210926
848480LV00009B/819
* 9 7 9 8 2 3 2 7 8 9 3 0 5 *